SPEAKING
as ONE

A LOOK
AT THE ECUMENICAL CREEDS

SCOTT HOEZEE

CRC Publications, Grand Rapids, Michigan
Wm. B. Eerdmans Publishing Co., Grand Rapids, Michigan

Cover photo: © PhotoDisc, Inc.

Unless otherwise indicated, the Scripture quotations in this publication are from the HOLY BIBLE, NEW INTERNATIONAL VERSION, © 1973, 1978, 1984, International Bible Society. Used by permission of Zondervan Bible Publishers.

Speaking as One: A Look at the Ecumenical Creeds, © 1997 by CRC Publications, 2850 Kalamazoo Ave. SE, Grand Rapids, MI 49560. Copublished by Wm. B. Eerdmans Publishing Co., Grand Rapids, MI 49503.

Printed in the United States of America on recycled paper. ✪ 1-800-333-8300 (US); 1-800-263-4252 (CAN)

Library of Congress Cataloging-in-Publication Data
Hoezee, Scott, 1964-
      Speaking as one: a look at the ecumenical creeds / Scott Hoezee.
        p.   cm.
      ISBN 1-56212-247-9 (alk. Paper)
      1. Creeds, Ecumenical. I. Title.
BT990.H64   1997
238'.1—dc21   973424
                                        CIP

10 9 8 7 6 5 4 3 2 1

CONTENTS

ACKNOWLEDGMENTS

So much of what I say and write—as well as the way I try to express it—can ultimately be traced back to the influence of my teacher, mentor, and friend, Neal Plantinga. In my years at Calvin Theological Seminary Neal's sparkling lectures taught me the value of precise yet creative theological thinking as well as the elegance of well-crafted words and carefully chosen illustrations. Anyone who has heard Neal preach or speak, anyone who has read his many wonderful articles and books knows what I mean.

Hence, in most everything I do, I owe Neal a debt of gratitude. In this particular project, however, all of that gets magnified several times. For nearly two decades ago, Neal, while completing his doctoral work at Princeton Seminary, composed an extremely helpful study on the ecumenical creeds and Reformed confessions entitled *A Place to Stand*. This current study is based squarely on that original book—indeed, it is essentially a reworking of it. Although I have reshaped and reshuffled some of the material, and although many of the illustrations are new, the core of this study remains very much the fruit of Neal's original research, work, and good writing.

As always, if there are deficits in this current study, they are wholly my fault. However, most of what is good in the pages ahead must be credited ultimately to Neal. My thanks to him also for asking me to be the writer for this revision and for the encouragement he gave as he peeked at various drafts of this work.

—Scott Hoezee

PREFACE

The Christian church has a language, and her creeds teach it to us. To be normal Christians we need not only a personal relationship with Jesus Christ through the power of the Holy Spirit, but also a working knowledge of the doctrine of Christ through the teaching of the holy Catholic church. After all, the Christian church is not an add-on to salvation, but an actual component of it. And the church's doctrinal talk about God, Christ, and salvation is not a nicety for advanced language students, but basic vocabulary for believers. In short (and with thanks to William Willimon), the creeds help us to "talk Christian."

In this crisp and lively introduction to the ecumenical creeds Scott Hoezee helps us learn our first language—the one that speaks of God, Christ, and salvation. This is a language known by believers across the world and along the centuries. This is a language that speaks the unspeakable mysteries of Trinity, incarnation, and atonement. This is a language that is always old and always new.

Jesus teaches us to love the Lord our God with all our mind—not just with our heart and soul and strength, but also with our *mind.* The point is that for us to learn how to "talk Christian" and, even more important, to "think Christian" shows not just that we are good students. It also shows that we are good lovers.

—Cornelius Plantinga, Jr.

THE END OF
CREEDS?

C reeds have fallen on hard times in the late twentieth century. For close to two millennia, Christians all over the world have believed, memorized, and even fought over statements like the Apostles' and Nicene creeds. But in the fast-paced and technologically dizzying world of the twentieth century, many see creeds in the same light as horse-drawn carriages and the pony express—relics of the past that are no longer necessary—only worthy of a historical footnote.

NO CREED BUT CHRIST

In all fairness, many who have contributed to this change in perspective have done so with good intentions. During the Roaring Twenties fundamentalist Christians tried to protect personal faith in the living Christ from what they saw as the

In *A Place to Stand* Cornelius Plantinga, Jr., observes that not only Christians have creeds. So do other faiths, including secular humanists. He cites Robert Ingersoll's four-article creed:

> Happiness is the only good.
> The place to be happy is here.
> The time to be happy is now.
> The way to be happy is to make others so.

deadly influences of liberalism. The fundamentalists wanted to differentiate themselves clearly from a brand of Christianity that in their view paid only lip-service to the faith by thoughtlessly reciting creeds in church—creeds really no longer even believed by those reciting them. In that same era confessional churches fought modernism by forbidding theater attendance, card playing, and dancing. Other Christians battled new teachings on evolution (a struggle epitomized by the Scopes "Monkey" Trial). But fundamentalist churches of that time carried on the battle against modernism by proclaiming that from then on they would embrace "no creed but Christ." They believed that the "no creed but Christ" banner would put some daylight between themselves and those they perceived to be theologically shaky.

A not-so-subtle implication of the "no creed but Christ" slogan is that creeds do not nurture lively faith. It suggests that creeds actually get in the way of real faith. In fact, in the staunchest fundamentalist churches, one can often find somewhere in the church's literature a "Statement" or "Summary of Beliefs" that looks suspiciously like a creed. But it is a local creed, not a broadly held ecumenical one. It is a homemade creed, not a traditional one. By writing their own statement instead of adopting the great formulas of the apostolic tradition, fundamentalist Christians claim distance from what they think has gone wrong in the modern church.

Traditional creeds suffered even harder times during and after the 1960s. Few decades in history have more successfully moved people away from established authority and traditional beliefs. The sixties ethos encouraged people to create new systems of belief based on personal experience alone, not on tradition. Where Christianity is concerned, a person's religious experiences and not the pronouncements of any church—past or present—become the measure of all things. The sixties gave rise to the "death of God" movement, which declares that God has somehow died, but graciously so. His death gives us all a chance to live life the way we see fit. We no longer have to obey the restrictions of God's commandments or will. Human beings are at last free to create new ideas, new patterns, new belief systems that better fit life in our helter-skelter modern

An oft-quoted creed during the sixties was spawned by mind-enhancing-drug advocate Dr. Timothy Leary. In three short phrases his creed signalled a lifestyle religiously embraced by a whole generation of young people—with disastrous results:

Tune in
Turn on
Drop out

world. Obviously a statement like the Nicene Creed did not fare well in this environment.

By the eighties the cultural dropouts of the sixties began to drop back in on culture. They started a massive return to the churches. The film of this anti-creedal thinking continued to coat the souls of these hippies, turned yuppies, turned religious seekers. What many of them wanted was a church that looked as unchurch-like as possible. Maintaining remnants of their 1960s dislike of tradition and established authority, they searched for churches that shelved formal doctrines and creeds in favor of new, contemporary, and pragmatic forms of worship, preaching, and teaching.

THE INFORMATION AGE

Still, as we approach the end of the millennium, you are holding in your hands a book designed to help you study the traditional ecumenical creeds. Doing so shows that you are open-minded enough to step back from our culture's excessive fascination with the present, take a second look at our common Christian past, and learn from it. You hope to connect with the church's history, which forms a fascinating part of God's history with his people. You sense that this history contains treasures that will enrich your faith. And you are right. But why?

Before we delve into each of the three ecumenical creeds, we will need to answer that question. We need to explain why it's useful for us, who live in the late twentieth century, to expend that kind of energy on these ancient confessions.

To begin answering that question we need to understand our own context. We live in an age when the marketplace of differing religious and moral ideas is much more diverse than it used to be and much closer to hand. The number of North Americans who profess to belong to a religion other than Christianity is on the rise. Muslims, for example, now number as high as ten million in the United States alone. Also on the rise are the numbers of people who adhere to a customized religion, a religion à la carte. These are religions that people

A foundational creed of Islam is comprehensive, memorable and *short:* Allah is God and Mohammed is his prophet.

make up for themselves, choosing and blending together elements of, say, Christianity, Hinduism, and New Age mysticism.

People today also have much greater access to diverse religious practices and ideas than they used to. Cables, wires, satellite dishes, and modems can now bring the world and its many options right into our homes. The information superhighway now runs through our front doors, exposing us, our children, and our young people to the welter of religious images, ideas, and practices currently in vogue. Whether they are actively clicking into an on-line chat room or passively soaking up music videos on MTV, our young people can now see, read, and hear more differing visions of reality than we could have dreamed of a generation or two ago.

KEEPING THE FAITH

Given this booming, buzzing new world of religious options, how will committed Christians keep the faith? Do we understand it? Can we explain it to others? Do we know the genuine articles of our faith well enough so that we can spot a counterfeit idea—even a good one—when we see it? Or are we content to go out into the religious confusion of our culture with only vague notions about what we believe to be true?

We have reason to worry on these fronts. Some time ago *Christianity Today,* a major Christian periodical, reported on a ministerial association that decided to allow a practicing witch into its group. When asked why and how they could do this, one clergyman claimed that the group could think of no compelling reason not to welcome the witch, especially since "we don't discriminate based on creed" (*Christianity Today,* Sept. 13, 1993). If you don't care about your own creed, you will not worry much about someone else's.

Meanwhile, sociologists are tracking the lifestyles and belief systems of the "baby boomers" and "baby busters." Many of them have been flocking back to church in the past fifteen years. The sociologists report that many seekers now possess an "almost theology." "Boomers" and "busters" are drawn to churches that place little emphasis on creeds and doctrines. So it's no surprise that the faith of many of them is an amalgam. Many claim that just feeling religious is more important than belonging to and participating in the life of a church. Some agree that while Jesus "works" for them, other people will find their ultimate destiny through Buddhism or Hinduism. Some add that orthodoxy in beliefs and morality is less important than respecting other people's freedom to choose their own beliefs and actions—to decide what is true and right for them.

William Willimon of Duke University Divinity School observes that anyone who claims that all religions say pretty much the same thing doesn't know much about other religions. For that matter, such a person doesn't know much about his or her own religion either. Not knowing much about even one's own religion is common today. This is a problem that cannot be solved simply by knowing the creeds of our Christian faith. But neither can it be solved without knowing them. Without knowing what Christians have long confessed in common, we cannot journey confidently and safely through the religious minefield of contemporary North America.

While the fundamentalists in earlier times professed to have "no creed but Christ," they did share many confessional statements. They did not say them, they sang them. They could still rely on a rich fund of Christian hymns and anthems to help them learn and confess their faith. Boomers, Busters and Generation Xers lack this important resource entirely.

THE MEASURE OF FAITH

From the beginning, creeds of varying kinds were designed as a norm or rule of faith. Like a carpenter's square, creeds help people take the measure of what is right and true and of what is crooked and untrue. Some of the first creed-like formulations can be traced all the way back to the earliest days of the Christian church.

The simplest and most powerful of these is the statement, "Jesus is Lord!" We have heard and said these words till they seem routine. But in the Mediterranean Basin of the first century, they made people gasp. After all, these words *rule out* Caesar and *rule in* Jesus. The first creed says what the gospel says: the crucified carpenter from Nazareth has been raised from the dead and now rules the world from his high place in heaven.

The early church also tried to capture the essentials of the faith in other phrases that believers could remember and pass along to others. In a day when having one's own copy of the Bible or any printed material was unheard of, believers needed small chunks of the gospel to carry with them. They needed something longer than "Jesus is Lord" and shorter than the entire Bible. "Jesus is Lord," while true and memorable, doesn't contain a very large portion of the faith. But the Scriptures—the complete rule for faith and life—are too long to memorize. So Christians in the early centuries of the church's life began to

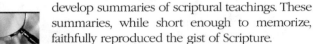

develop summaries of scriptural teachings. These summaries, while short enough to memorize, faithfully reproduced the gist of Scripture.

Many commentators believe that Philippians 2:6-11 and 2 Timothy 2:11-13 are such early church hymns or creeds, which people could memorize and which the apostle Paul, in turn, quotes approvingly in his letters. By the time Paul composes what may be among his last letters, the pastoral letters (1 Timothy, 2 Timothy, and Titus), there are lots of such "faithful sayings" to call on. Often in these epistles Paul states, "Here is a trustworthy saying," and then goes on to quote a few lines of a then-current summary of the gospel. His fellow Christians knew these and carried them with them in their hearts. Because Paul included these sayings in his letters, they have become a part of what we now call the New Testament. In fact, these summarizing creeds came first and the Bible came later.

One intriguing idea suggests that we should also look at early Christian art as a vehicle for such brief and memorable creeds. Mosaic tile floors of ancient near-Eastern churches and catacomb walls in Rome display numerous works of art that reflect common confessional themes. Jesus is frequently depicted as our Good Shepherd. The sharing of bread and wine at communion confesses the believers' fellowship with their Lord and with each other. This indicates that we can say creeds, but we can also see them.

CREEDAL CONTRIBUTIONS

These early sayings, as well as the later creeds of the church, served several purposes: for identification, unification, education, edification, and for apologetics.

Creeds help to *identify* Christian beliefs and the people who hold them. Christians are those who know and believe what these statements contain. In a world in which Christianity was a new minority religion competing with other religions, Christians needed to be able to spot each other. Creeds help to identify and *unify* Christian believers. Anyone, anywhere, who knew and accepted the same creeds could safely be embraced as a fellow believer.

A very early Christian creed that identified people as Christians is the sentence "I believe in Jesus Christ, the Son of God, our Savior." The early Christians even developed a symbol to remind them of this creed: a fish. Each letter of the

Greek word for "fish," *ichthus,* stands for the key words of this creed. The first one, the Greek letter *iota* is also the first letter in the Greek spelling of the name "Jesus." The second letter, the Greek letter *chi,* is the first letter of the word for "Christ," and so forth. So the letters of *ichthus* stand for the words "Jesus Christ, God's Son, Savior." After a while, the mere outline of the fish was enough to deliver the goods to those in the know. Anyone displaying the fish identified himself or herself as a fellow Christian. Even today modern Christians still display this ancient sign on bumper stickers, pins, signs, and necklaces.

Hippolytus, a third-century bishop, gives this account of a typical baptism in Rome: "When the person being baptized goes down into the water, he who baptizes him, putting his hand on him, shall say: 'Do you believe in God, the Father Almighty?' And the person shall say: 'I believe.' Then holding his hand on his head, he shall baptize him once. And then he shall say: 'Do you believe in Christ Jesus, the Son of God?' . . . And when he says: 'I believe,' he is baptized again. And again he shall say: 'Do you believe in the Holy Spirit, in the holy church, and the resurrection of the body?' The person being baptized shall say: 'I believe,' and then he is baptized a third time."

TEACHING AIDS

Creeds not only identify believers in the world, they also *educate* and *edify* believers within the church. So the early church used creeds to prepare converts for baptism. A person who was to be baptized into the name of the Father and of the Son and of the Holy Spirit had to know who these persons are and what they have done. The early church also used creeds to build up the faith of baptized members during worship services.

Creedal summaries also serve a third function in our world of competing ideas: an *apologetic* and polemical one. The church uses these summaries to counter false notions in the wider world and wrongheaded ideas within the church. Knowing the creeds helps believers sort out right ideas from wrong ones and equips them to defend their own beliefs against competing opinions. Also, today in our increasingly diverse marketplace of ideas, creeds distinguish real Christians from pseudo-Christians. They unite true believers around the Bible's core teachings. They educate seekers in the essentials of the faith and build up believers so that they are able to combat false teachings.

CREEDAL CONNECTIONS

Another benefit we receive from knowing and studying the creeds is an enlarged sense of the church. Creeds connect us not only to the Scriptures but also to the broad communion of the saints. The creeds express what all our brothers and sisters, from a variety of cultures, confess and celebrate throughout the world today. And the creeds also express what our brothers and sisters throughout the whole of Christian history have thought, believed, and confessed—including the church's

best theologians. When we are able to speak as they spoke and to believe as they believed, we join the church of all ages in celebrating its common foundation, Jesus Christ, our Lord. When we deliberately speak the same language of our Christian ancestors, we remind ourselves that the church is larger than any one generation.

Let's not underestimate this need for a common language of faith. In a popular series of children's books we follow the adventures of Frank and Ernest, an elephant and a bear who from time to time get asked to fill in for baseball announcers, truck drivers, and other specialized workers. In each story Frank and Ernest discover that to do their new job well, they need to know its practices. They also need to know its language and jargon. To become good baseball announcers, for instance, Frank and Ernest need to know what a "sacrifice" is, what "a frozen rope" means (a line drive), and what it means for a batter to hit "a can of corn" (an easy-to-catch pop-up). In each story Frank and Ernest realize that by learning the language of a profession, they are joining an already-existing community whose history predates them, a community that will continue to exist after them.

Creeds are the language of our first vocation, Christianity. They help us to speak its language intelligently. By knowing these statements we connect with God's people and with God's Spirit, who promises always to be leading the church into all truth. Of course, the creeds need fresh applications and explanations for each new generation. But for centuries Christians have believed that what gets applied and explained afresh is the truth of Scripture as it comes to us in the summary form of creeds.

A particularly moving way in which churches sometimes celebrate the rich diversity with which God has blessed them is to invite members from different ethnic backgrounds to recite a creed or confessional statement in the language of their place of origin. While most worshipers might not understand the words, their common knowledge of the creed means that they know what's being said. In that way their shared creed takes them back very close to the Pentecost experience of a diversity of languages celebrating a common, Spirit-gifted understanding.

ONE IN FAITH

Early church believers in places like Philippi, Ephesus, and Corinth presented new converts to what for them was a new religion. They needed to make sense of their new-found faith in the wake of what they once believed and in sensitive, sometimes risky, inter-action with the beliefs of their non-Christian neighbors, coworkers, and family members. As they tried to make their way in the world, these early Christians were strengthened, edified, and united by being able to tell each other the truth of the gospel in creedal form. By knowing these sayings the early church was formed and united in a common faith, hope, and identity within a culture and religious setting at least as diverse as our own.

The creeds of the Christian church have often had this uniting effect, especially during times of crisis when the church especially needs to reaffirm its most central beliefs. At such times the church looks for the breath of God in Scripture, even as Scripture is captured for us in the creeds. Today we are blessed to possess three sturdy and rich creeds: the Apostles', Nicene, and Athanasian creeds. Each is embraced by almost every Christian group in the world, reaching across denomi-national lines and national boundaries. These creeds have stood the test of time. They have been approved by generation after generation of believers and accepted as accurate sum-maries of what God tells us in Scripture. They offer us rich, nourishing insights, as in the following units we examine each of them more closely.

Creedal elements routinely find their way into the liturgy of the church. In the fourth century Saint Basil, bishop of Caesarea, took a great deal of flak when he modified a formula used routinely in wor-ship at that time. A standard for-mula in the Greek churches was: "Glory *to* the Father *through* the Son *in* the Holy Spirit." Basil al-tered it to "Glory *to* the Father *with* the Son together *with* the Holy Spirit." The seemingly innocent substitution of a few prepositions caused such a flap because Saint Basil from that time on had his parishioners weekly glorifying not only the Father but also the Son and the Holy Spirit. Since all agreed that only God may be wor-shiped, this little formula implicitly confessed that all three persons mentioned are, in fact, truly God— a concept that was hotly disputed at the time.

R E F L E C T I O N S

*I*f you are using this book in a class or small group setting, this section offers some quotes and questions that
may help guide the discussion. Participants could take
turns reading the quotes from the text out loud and explain them briefly before inviting input from the others.
The questions prompt group members to go beyond the
material presented here to explore its relevance to their
lives. If you're reading this book on your own, you may
wish to take some time to mull over these sections as well.

▶ *Points to Ponder*

*In the fast-paced and technologically dizzying world of the
twentieth century, many see creeds in the same light as
horse-drawn carriages and the pony express—relics of the
past that are no longer necessary.*

*The sixties ethos encouraged people to create new systems
of belief based on personal experience alone, not on tradition. Where Christianity is concerned, a person's religious experiences and not the pronouncements of any
church—past or present—become the measure of all
things.*

*Some ["boomers" and "busters"] add that orthodoxy in be-
liefs and morality is less important than respecting other
people's freedom to choose their own beliefs and actions—
to decide what is true and right for them.*

*Without knowing what Christians have long confessed in
common, we cannot journey confidently and safely
through the religious minefield of contemporary North
America.*

*When we deliberately speak the same language of our
Christian ancestors, we remind ourselves that the church
is larger than any one generation.*

▶ Implications and Applications

1. What did the fundamentalists mean by contending that we should have "no creed but Christ"? Do you agree? Why or why not?

2. Should we continue to use creeds even if they deter people from rejoining our church?

3. What do you personally hope to gain by examining the creeds?

4. Of the many uses for the creeds, which do you consider the most important? Explain.

5. What are some fresh ways we can use the creeds today?

APOSTLES' CREED

I believe in God, the Father almighty,
  creator of heaven and earth.

I believe in Jesus Christ, his only Son, our Lord,
  who was conceived by the Holy Spirit
  and born of the virgin Mary.
  He suffered under Pontius Pilate,
  was crucified, died, and was buried;
  he descended into hell.
  The third day he rose again from the dead.
  He ascended to heaven
  and is seated at the right hand of God the Father almighty.
  From there he will come to judge the living and the dead.

I believe in the Holy Spirit,
  the holy catholic church,
  the communion of saints,
  the forgiveness of sins,
  the resurrection of the body,
  and the life everlasting. Amen.

THE
APOSTOLIC CREED
A Rare Vintage

S ome drinks are made to be gulped, others to be sipped. On a hot summer day a cold glass of lemonade does its job best if we knock it back pretty fast. But other drinks should be savored. A well-aged wine, for example, is meant to be enjoyed slowly, allowing its richness to coat our palate and warm our innards. Such a drink is the result of years of labor. Slow enjoyment of a good wine shows our respect for the work that produced it and our desire to enjoy fully the fruit of that work.

Roman Catholic writer Joseph S. Hogan cautions us that the Apostles' Creed should never be recited quickly: "That's gulping down a well-aged Mouton-Rothschild like a nickel soda. Say each phrase slowly; it can take a lifetime just to grasp the first four words" (*Context*, July 15, 1995).

It took many lifetimes to get this creed fermented, clarified, and aged just right. As we will see, centuries of agonizing biblical and theological work lie behind even its simplest lines.

So we should savor it, especially because the Apostles' Creed presents timeless truths that connect us with our Savior. Sad to say, we often "gulp" this creed instead. Familiarity breeds contempt. Or maybe in this case it just makes us thoughtless. Maybe we are like people who have been raised alongside a vineyard and who have tasted good wine every day for years—even a truly fine vintage no longer impresses us.

Maybe we treat the Apostles' Creed in the same way. We have recited it so often that we overlook its genius. We no longer think of the prayer that went into its composition. One person who was thinking of the creed and of our routine repetition of it has remarked that, in a sense, the Apostles' Creed is a kind of martyr. It has died for the faith! So in one way we may know the creed all too well, while in another way we may know very little about it.

For instance, we may have memorized the Apostles' Creed and yet have little idea of its history. We may feel at home with the creed but feel embarrassed if someone asks us a question about how Jesus "descended into hell." In this unit we will remind ourselves of the history behind what some call "the creed of creeds." We will also dip into a few of its articles to demonstrate that there is more here than meets the eye. Then we'll explore some possible uses for the creed. These will bring out some of the richness of this wonderful document. For in the end we want to propose that the Apostles' Creed represents a rare theological and biblical vintage worth savoring.

BEGINNINGS

Many Christians throughout the ages have assumed that this creed was written by the apostles themselves, with each apostle perhaps contributing one line. This is because it has been known for centuries as "The Apostles' Creed," and because it can be broken down into twelve lines, presumably one for each apostle. However, though this creed is very old, there is no evidence that the apostles themselves composed any of it. Still, its name is appropriate. Its teachings reflect an accurate summary of the apostles' authoritative teachings—the legacy on which the church is founded.

For fun, do a quick tally of how many times you've said the Apostles' Creed. Then give a rough "guesstimate" of how many times it's been recited around the globe since it first came into being. After all that reciting you'd think we'd know it well. Guess again. For example, most people think that the article of the creed confessing that Jesus "descended into hell" is referring to the place of eternal judgment. It isn't. The original word used for *hell* is *Hades*. It's the place all people good or bad were thought to go to when they die. The *hell* we think of is referred to by a different name: *Gehenna*. See a Bible dictionary to explore the differences between these terms. Then take another look at what the Apostles' Creed is really confessing.

The Apostles' Creed can be traced as far back as the second and third centuries. As we saw in chapter 1, early Christian believers needed handy summaries of the faith that they could memorize and carry with them in their hearts. Among these summaries was a baptismal creed based on the Great Commission of Matthew 28. After being instructed in the gospel of the Triune God, early Christian baptismal candidates were asked, "Do you believe in God the Father?"

The candidate would respond with the Latin "Credo," which means, "I believe."

"Do you believe in God the Son?"

"I believe."

"Do you believe in God the Holy Spirit?"

"I believe."

Following this three-fold *credo,* from which we derive the word "creed," the new believer would receive baptism.

Eventually this trinitarian baptismal creed appears to be expanded into a short statement. Asked to state his or her faith, the candidate for baptism responded, "I believe in God the Father Almighty, and in Jesus Christ, his only Son, our Lord, and in the Holy Spirit, the holy church, the resurrection of the flesh." By A.D. 340 the church in Rome had adopted a creedal statement that became known as *R,* or the Roman Creed. When we read *R,* we easily discover that it is the immediate ancestor of the Apostles' Creed:

1. *I believe in God Almighty*
2. *and in Christ Jesus, his only Son, our Lord*
3. *who was born of the Holy Spirit and the Virgin Mary*
4. *who was crucified under Pontius Pilate and was buried*
5. *and the third day rose from the dead*
6. *who ascended into heaven*
7. *and sitteth on the right hand of the Father*
8. *whence he cometh to judge the living and the dead*
9. *and in the Holy Ghost*
10. *the holy church*
11. *the remission of sins*

When we look at the Apostles' Creed, we discover an interesting paradox. Vintage creeds like this one were pressed into existence by the constant squeeze put on biblical teaching by false doctrines. These heresies existed from the beginning and were widespread. When belief is repeatedly buffeted by false teaching, over time history produces a mature, robust, fragrant confession that clearly and elegantly expresses the Truth. The process parallels that of the horrific persecutions that also shook the early church but caused it to emerge lean, strong, and deeply committed to its Lord.

12. *the resurrection of the flesh*
13. *the life everlasting.*

THE FINISHED PRODUCT

The Apostles' Creed was crafted into its present form by about A.D. 700 after several more centuries of thought, discussion, prayer, and study. As we can see by studying it, the creed is structured according to the three persons of the Holy Trinity. It is oriented toward salvation and centers on Jesus Christ and the key events of his ministry. The overall sweep of the creed moves from creation through redemption and on into the new creation of everlasting life.

The idea that the apostles actually wrote this creed arose early and remained firmly in place until the time of the Renaissance. An Italian, Lorenzo Valla (1405-1457), founder of historical criticism, finally debunked this fondly-held misconception.

All creeds are, by nature, selections of biblical and theological material. The purpose of such statements is to give believers the doctrinal essentials of the faith without all the details. That is why some things—God as Creator, Jesus as Lord, the resurrection of the body—get included in the creed, while others—the story of Melchizedek, David's affair with Bathsheba, the Parable of the Sower—get left out. A creed doesn't have room for everything. We couldn't memorize it if it did.

CREEDAL GAPS?

If the Apostles' Creed wants to give us the essentials of our faith, then why does it leave out most of the Old Testament? The doctrine of creation does get mentioned, but nothing of covenant, or of promise and fulfillment, or of the Exodus. The doctrine of justification by faith alone, which John Calvin called "the hinge of the Reformation," is also missing. So is explicit teaching of our Lord's atonement for our sins. On the other hand, the creed takes precious space for Pontius Pilate. How does a second-rate Roman governor, scarcely mentioned even in secular histories of that era, get mentioned in a creed in which not even Abraham or Paul show up? As someone once cleverly phrased the question, why is the entire life and ministry of Jesus packed into the comma between "born of the virgin Mary" and "suffered under Pontius Pilate"?

We can grant that a creed cannot begin to re-hearse all that Jesus did while on earth. But can the Apostles' Creed not say *something* about his life? If we could fill in the blank, what would we choose to mention?

This may be a good time to pause and reflect a moment on that question. If you could revise the Apostles' Creed, what *would* you put in that comma between "born of the virgin Mary" and "suffered under Pontius Pilate"?

Scholars do not know precisely why this creed mentions some events but leaves others out. We do know that at least a few of the inclusions reflect issues of the era in which the creed itself is compiled. For example, at the time of its forma-tion a battle was raging between Christians and people called Gnostics, who took a dim view of physical reality. Gnostics con-tended that only spiritual reality is worthy of our interest. They claimed that during Jesus' earthly ministry his body was mere-ly a costume that he slipped over the top of his divine nature. Like Clark Kent, who looks like a mild-mannered reporter but who is really Superman, Jesus only *looked* like a man from Nazareth but was really, only and always, a divine superbeing. To combat this heresy, those who composed the creed made certain to include biblical items such as Jesus' birth, suffering, death, and burial. These all point to Jesus' true humanity.

REMEMBER!

By reciting the main deeds of Christ the creed's authors did more than defeat heretics. They had something else in view as well. They knew Scripture, so they knew that when believ-ers want to tell of the saving work of God, they start reciting what God has done. They tell of God's great, saving deeds. This means that we should think of a Bible book like Deuteronomy as providing the motivation for the middle section of the creed. Deuteronomy regularly rehearses and retells God's saving acts in history. The watchword of Deuteronomy for the people of Israel is "Remember and do not forget." This is a lesson the creed's authors took to heart.

We can think as well of Peter's great sermon in Acts 2. On Pentecost, Peter gives the historical background for the excite-ment that has come upon the church. It centers in the nature and acts of Christ, about whom Peter says:

- *Jesus is the Christ*
- *Jesus is the Lord*
- *he performed mighty acts*
- *he was wickedly crucified*
- *but God raised him from the dead*
- *he has ascended into heaven*
- *he sends his Holy Spirit to all who have been "called out" from the world into Christ's fellowship*
- *we must be baptized into Christ for the forgiveness of sins and for salvation*

Here we find a biblical sketch that reminds us of the middle section of the Apostles' Creed, which deals with Christ, and also with the creed's final section, which deals with the Holy Spirit and the Spirit's gifts: fellowship, forgiveness of sins, and life everlasting.

DECLARED INNOCENT

So why does the creed remind us that Jesus was crucified "under Pontius Pilate"? After all, Pilate is only a minor biblical figure.

Perhaps because the mention of Pilate, a secular magistrate, firmly anchors the trial and death of Jesus in world history. Or maybe, as Calvin thought, the creed wants us to see that Jesus not only *was* innocent, but was also *found innocent* by a civil magistrate. This clearly witnesses to the fact that his crucifixion was unjust.

Jesus was condemned to die as if he were guilty, even though he clearly was not—a fact that has theological importance beyond anything Pilate could have guessed.

In its reflection on the Apostles' Creed (Lord's Day 38), the Heidelberg Catechism makes the point elegantly:

Why did [Christ] suffer "under Pontius Pilate" as judge?
So that he,
 though innocent,
might be condemned by a civil judge,
and so free us from the severe judgment of God
 that was to fall on us.

PAUSING TO PONDER

As we have seen, each article in the Apostles' Creed represents a theological distillate of the ages. Each article is the boiled-down version of a lot of deep biblical scholarship.

In this study we cannot pause to ponder each article, but we do want to present some especially remarkable ones.

Consider the article about "Jesus Christ . . . our Lord." In the early church the statement "Jesus is Lord!" is a three-word summary of the entire gospel. It delivers a powerful, shocking message. Pious Jews hear in that line the worst kind of sin. From Old Testament times only Yahweh is confessed as Lord; he alone is the one true God. Bending the knee before any other lord is clearly blasphemy. Yet the early Christians confess that Jesus possesses the authority of Yahweh. Peter makes this transfer already at Pentecost. First he quotes Joel 2, "Everyone who calls on the name of [Yahweh] will be saved" (Acts 2:21). But now, shockingly and blasphemously to Jewish ears, Peter proclaims that God has made "this man" (v. 23), "this Jesus"— the very one they crucified—"both Lord and Christ" (v. 36).

Peter jolts Roman listeners too. He makes a treasonous statement: "Jesus is Lord." In the Roman Empire only Caesar was recognized as *deus et dominus,* "god and lord." All citizens were commanded to give him, and him alone, their highest allegiance. But early Christians refused to give Augustus or Nero or Caligula any ultimate allegiance because they knew that *Jesus* is the Lord of all lords. The believers' refusal to bow to the emperor's claim makes their lives and their faith dangerous until the reign of Constantine in the fourth century. So when the Romans hear "Jesus is Lord," they gasp at its blatantly treasonous ring.

Today the word "Lord" and the phrases "Praise the Lord" and "Jesus is Lord" roll off our tongues fairly easily. But we ought to think over what we are saying. By professing Jesus as our *Lord* we proclaim that Jesus is no dead hero. We confess that he remains alive—almost frighteningly alive—and he claims every square inch of this world and every ounce of loyalty from our hearts. No doubt Jesus wants our praise. But he also demands our obedience: in our parenting, our use of money, our family's use of video technology, and in our racial and gender relationships. Do we really want to praise the Lord? Or is that just pep rally talk?

EMBODIED HOPE

Often we fail to appreciate the impact of two other articles as well: "the resurrection of the body," and "the life everlasting." Because they come at the tail end of the creed, we may gulp

Again, the Heidelberg Catechism (Lord's Day 13) expands so elegantly on what the Apostles' Creed confesses:

Why do you call [Jesus] "our Lord"?
Because—
    not with gold or silver,
    but with his precious blood—
he has set us free
    from sin and from the tyranny of the devil,
and has bought us,
    body and soul,
to be his very own.

down these two articles even faster than the others. Yet these articles contain a major part of our Christian hope. They center it on a truly mind-boggling event: One day bodies from all over the world will be reconstructed for their owners and restored to them. Like Christ, who rose on the third day, we shall rise—not to float around like Caspar the Friendly Ghost, but to stride, swim, dance, sing, and drink wine with Jesus.

When heaven descends to earth (Rev. 21:1-4) and God dwells with us here, then we will need bodies. We will need and receive good ones, high quality bodies like Jesus' resurrected body. This is exciting enough for most of us: the chance one day to eat and drink with Jesus, maybe even to swim with the whales and fly with the eagles. But imagine what it means for brothers and sisters who in this life have had to put up with disease or disfigurement!

A USABLE CREED

Down through the centuries Christians have found many uses for the Apostles' Creed. In the early church it provided a good summary of what then appeared to be a new religion. It served believers as an excellent springboard for evangelism and witness and enabled them to answer questions about their faith.

As always, the creed remains a useful tool for teaching new converts. Here, after all, is the church's summary of essentials from Scripture. For the same reason, the creed provides a rich resource for the preaching and teaching ministry of the church. That's why it also appears, article for article, in other confessional documents such as the Heidelberg Catechism as well.

Christians also use the creed as a testament of faith at funerals. When we stand before a grave alongside the body of a loved one, we say words that bring the weight of centuries to us. We stand together and confess, "The third day he rose again from the dead." Then we add, "I believe in the resurrection of the body and the life everlasting. Amen."

In worship believers use the Apostles' Creed as a reminder of the faith and as a response to God's presence. The creed fits well at a baptism, especially at the baptism of an adult. It also

Eerdmans' Handbook to the History of Christianity points out that the specific purpose for creedal statements changed radically: "The old creeds were creeds for converts, the new creed was a creed for bishops. The old creeds had been local, the new one was to be universally binding. It took over from the old *Rule of Faith* as a test of orthodoxy" (p. 115).

provides a fitting act of worship at our celebration of the Lord's Supper. Sometimes we use the creed to follow the sermon as a kind of congregational "Amen!" to the Word that is preached. When the gospel is proclaimed we can stand up and confirm that we believe it by reciting the creed together.

The Apostles' Creed is fine wine. We ought to savor this treasure of our faith. When we do, when we say it faithfully, we are not merely *describing* a vow. We are actually *making* one. Just as we would never say "I do" at a wedding without giving the matter some careful thought, so we must never say "I believe" without the full weight of our minds and hearts.

Having savored this fine product of our Christian heritage, we'll move on in the next unit to sample a creed of a similar, but slightly different vintage: the Nicene Creed. Although it has a different flavor, we'll discover that it has aged equally well.

R E F L E C T I O N S

▶ *Points to Ponder*

Joseph S. Hogan cautions us that the Apostles' Creed should never be recited quickly: "That's gulping down a well-aged Mouton-Rothschild like a nickel soda. Say each phrase slowly; it can take a lifetime just to grasp the first four words" (Context, July 15, 1995).

[The Apostles' Creed's] name is appropriate. Its teachings reflect an accurate summary of the apostles' authoritative teachings—the legacy on which the church is founded.

The creed is structured according to the three persons of the Holy Trinity. It is oriented toward salvation, and centered on Jesus Christ and the key events of his ministry. The overall sweep of the creed moves from creation through redemption and on into the new creation of everlasting life.

Why is the entire life and ministry of Jesus packed into the comma between "born of the virgin Mary" and "suffered under Pontius Pilate"?

In the early church the statement "Jesus is Lord!" is a three-word summary of the entire gospel. It delivers a powerful, shocking message.

The Apostles' Creed is fine wine. We ought to savor this treasure of our faith. When we do, when we say it faithfully, we are not merely describing a vow. We are actually making one.

▶ Implications and Applications

1. How has the Apostles' Creed become a martyr for the faith?

2. How does your congregation use the Apostles' Creed in worship? Do you have any suggestions for changes in this area?

3. What does the confession "Jesus is Lord" really mean? What concrete implications does it have for your life?

4. What would you add to this creed that you consider essential to the faith? What would you "weed out"?

5. How can the Apostles' Creed be of use to you in sharing the Christian faith with people who don't know it?

NICENE CREED

We believe in one God,
the Father almighty,
maker of heaven and earth,
of all things visible and invisible.

And in one Lord Jesus Christ,
the only Son of God,
begotten from the Father before all ages,
God from God,
Light from Light,
true God from true God,
begotten, not made;
of the same essence as the Father.
Through him all things were made.
For us and for our salvation
he came down from heaven;
he became incarnate by the Holy Spirit and the
virgin Mary,
and was made human.
He was crucified for us under Pontius Pilate;
he suffered and was buried.
The third day he rose again, according to the Scriptures.
He ascended to heaven
and is seated at the right hand of the Father.
He will come again with glory
to judge the living and the dead.
His kingdom will never end.

And we believe in the Holy Spirit,
the Lord, the giver of life.
He proceeds from the Father and the Son,
and with the Father and the Son is worshiped and glorified.
He spoke through the prophets.
We believe in one holy catholic and apostolic church.
We affirm one baptism for the forgiveness of sins.
We look forward to the resurrection of the dead,
and to life in the world to come. Amen.

THE
NICENE
CREED

Who Is Jesus?

I n one remarkable week in the spring of 1996 all three of the United States' major newsmagazines ran cover stories about Jesus. *Time, Newsweek,* and *U.S. News & World Report* each put a painting of Jesus on their cover, accompanied by the question: Who is Jesus? Although they coincided with that year's Holy Week, the main spur for these stories was the Jesus Seminar and its radical reworking of the New Testament's witness to Jesus.

Founded in 1985, the Jesus Seminar is a group of scholars who claim that their academic work demonstrates that 82 percent of the words attributed to Jesus in Matthew, Mark, Luke, and John were never actually spoken by him at all. Seminar participants contend that the gospel writers invented these sayings to substantiate their religious claims that Jesus is the divine Son of God. The Jesus Seminar goes beyond casting doubt on the words of the Bible. It contends that the real Jesus was no more than a curious traveling preacher from Nazareth, the very human son of Mary and Joseph. At best, these scholars claim, Jesus taught some rather novel things that landed him in trouble with the Roman and Jewish authorities. They ended up killing him on a cross. His body was then dumped in a shallow pauper's grave where it was devoured by a pack of wild dogs.

FROM WHICH SIDE?

Jesus once asked his disciples, "Who do people say that I am?" The disciples' answer reveals a diversity of answers to that question. The diversity has only increased in the millennia since. The controversy swirling around the Jesus Seminar reveals that many people today retain a very lively interest in Jesus' identity and arrive at widely varying conclusions. The main question with which the Jesus Seminar challenges people is this: From whose side does Jesus come? Does he come from God's side, from heaven as *very God of very God,* or was he no more than a human being, conceived by the sexual union of Joseph and Mary? The Jesus Seminar clearly concludes the latter.

Their critics rightly point out that the participants in this Seminar are not an objective group. These scholars do not represent a broad spectrum of theological thinkers. They all proceed from a liberal tradition that does not believe in Jesus as the actual, historical Son of God. The methods by which they supposedly debunk all but 18 percent of Jesus' gospel words reflect their deep biases. Their procedures are so influenced by these biases that the Seminar's conclusions of necessity echo their presuppositions.

A good thing resulting from this debate is that people are forced to ponder afresh what Christians have always known to be the key issue: the true origin and identity of Jesus. Does he come directly from God as the very Son of God? Or is Jesus' origin restricted to this earth, the same as everyone else's? If the former case is true, then Christians can go on worshiping Jesus, praying to Jesus, expecting salvation from Jesus. If the latter is true, then all of that is bankrupt, idolatrous, foolish, and utterly hopeless.

Look at the variety of answers to this question already found during Jesus' earthly ministry:

[13][Jesus] asked his disciples, "Who do people say the Son of Man is?" [14]They replied, "Some say John the Baptist; others say Elijah; and still others, Jeremiah or one of the prophets" (Matt. 16:13-14).

What would lead the people of Jesus' day to mistake him for those mentioned?

Because the question of who Jesus is, is so vitally important, it's no surprise that answering it is a chief concern of the earliest theologians in the Christian church. In the fourth century A.D. the Roman Emperor himself intervenes in this Jewish concern by calling a theological conference to settle the matter once and for all.

THE BURNING QUESTION

Starting around A.D. 318, a man named Arius, an astute but misguided theological thinker, began to teach that Jesus is no more than a creation of God the Father. Jesus is a superior life form, to be sure, far superior to human beings and even to angels. But he is a creature, made by the Father in a way somehow reminiscent of God's other acts of creation. The Son of God has a definable beginning. He is neither fully God nor fully human. He is a third kind of entity, the likes of which has never before existed and will never come into being again. By teaching this, Arius hoped to head off what he perceived to be a dangerous polytheism. After all, he asked, if we say that the Father is God and Jesus is God, and if we worship both the Father and the Son, don't we worship two different gods? If so, isn't that utterly wrong and unbiblical?

Arius's question unleashed a storm of controversy in the ancient world of the Roman Empire. Just as the Jesus Seminar provokes wide discussion about Jesus today, so in the fourth century the work of Arius attracted a lot of attention. Talk about Jesus becomes all the rage in the marketplace, the buzz of conversation in pubs and restaurants, and a regular feature on the Op-Ed pages. Therefore Emperor Constantine, himself a convert to Christianity, ended up convening the Council of Nicea in A.D. 325. As many as 318 Christian thinkers and scholars from around the then-known world met in the city of Nicea to ponder the biblical teachings on Jesus and to weigh Arius's claims in the theological balance.

To put it mildly, things did not go well for Arius. He was condemned and his teachings anathematized—cursed. The bulk of this council's pronouncements can still be read today in the Nicene Creed. It declares that Jesus is "begotten, not made, of the same essence as the Father." In other words, Jesus

It's astounding to discover that in three centuries the Christian faith, although mercilessly reviled and persecuted for all that time, spreads itself empire-wide and becomes so culturally dominant that the chief civic ruler convenes this important church meeting. If you look carefully you may find a phrase or two in the Nicene Creed that helps you to identify the reason for this.

and the Father are one and the same God, sharing a common, core essence. As such, Jesus the Son can no more have a created beginning than can God the Father. Father and Son are made of the same eternal, divine "stuff." They are distinct persons but only one God. The Council of Nicea roundly condemned as a horrible heresy any suggestion that there is a radical difference between the Father and the Son in terms of origin, being, power, or essence. It excommunicated Arius from the church along with those who embraced his teachings.

A CAREFUL CREED

When we recite the Nicene Creed, it is not difficult to detect its precise language and careful wording. This creed is quite a bit longer than the Apostles' Creed, which dispenses with the identity of Jesus in just three words, "his only Son." The difference between them is largely due to the Nicene Creed's more rigorous task of identifying Jesus as the fully divine Son of God. While it shares a trinitarian structure with the Apostles' Creed and is similarly salvation-oriented, the Nicene Creed takes much greater pains to stake down who Jesus is.

Actually, the Nicene Creed is the product of more than just one early church council. We can trace the bulk of it back to the Council of Nicea in A.D. 325. But this confession did not reach its final form until A.D. 451, following two more major theological symposia: the Council of Constantinople in A.D. 381 and the landmark Council of Chalcedon in A.D. 451. These last two councils continued to wrestle with issues related to the doctrine of the Trinity. They struggled to achieve a biblical understanding of the full divinity of the Holy Spirit. They also dealt further with questions of how to make sense of Christ's becoming a human being.

Among the key lines of the final form of the Nicene Creed is this one: "begotten from the Father before all ages . . ." This clearly refutes Arius's idea that the Son of God was created within time like other creatures. To be certain that it has firmly nailed shut the lid on the coffin of Arius's heresy, the creed adds: "begotten, not made, of the same essence as the Father . . ." The English words "of the same essence" stem from a single Greek word, *homoousios*. That one word has ever since distinguished an orthodox Christian in good standing from a heretic worthy of excommunication. While the creed confesses Jesus to be *homoousios,* "of the same essence" as God, the camp of Arius claims that Jesus is only *homoiousios,* "of a similar essence."

A BIG DIFFERENCE

Those who criticize the modern-day use of the creeds often allege that the antiquity of these documents limits their usefulness in the modern world. They consider the Arian controversy a classic case in point. Who cares that people sixteen hundred years ago debated these fine points of trinitarian teaching? As one cynical historian puts it, the whole world back then was in an uproar over a single diphthong, over two letters in the middle of that strange little Greek word. So why should we care about that now?

The fact that three major American periodicals put Jesus on their covers indicates that a lot of people are still interested in this very point. And rightly so. Consider what was at stake back then and what remains at stake now.

The early Christians, like Christians today, worshiped Jesus as God. They sang hymns to him, offered up prayers in his name, and looked to him as their Sovereign Lord, from whom they expected their very salvation. But Arius taught that Jesus is not God but is only *like* God. The Jesus Seminar scholars espouse even more radical teachings. If they are right, then all such Christian practices amount to overblown optimism at best and blatant idolatry at worst. Christians past and present have no business worshiping Jesus if he is not "God from God, Light from Light, true God from true God." If Jesus is just another creature like angels, humans, or hummingbirds, then Christians have reason to doubt whether he was actually strong enough to take on sin and the devil—to pull off the cosmic feat of achieving our salvation. If Jesus is not truly and really our eternal God, then a great deal of the New Testament is ill-focused, overly optimistic, and blasphemous in the claims it makes about him.

If you think the language of the Nicene Creed referring to Christ is difficult, try that of the Council of Chalcedon, as it finally formulates the position summarized in the Nicene Creed and adopted by the Christian church ever since:

"We . . . teach men to confess one and the same Son, our Lord Jesus Christ, the same perfect in Godhead and also perfect in manhood; truly God and truly man, of a reasonable soul and body; consubstantial (homoousion) with the Father according to the Godhead, and consubstantial with us according to the manhood . . . one and the same Christ, Son, Lord, Only-begotten, in two natures, inconfusedly, unchangeably, indivisibly, inseparably, the distinction of natures being by no means taken away by the union, but rather the property of each nature being preserved, and concurring in one person (prosopon) and one subsistence (hypostasis), not parted or divided into two persons, but one and the same Son and Only-begotten, God the Word, the Lord Jesus Christ. . . ."

—A History of the Christian Church, p. 139

JESUS TODAY

Today we need to consider some other wrinkles as well. It's true that outside of the circle of trained ministers and theologians, most people are not pondering Greek terminology. But many people are still trying to make sense of Jesus. Some very wrong ideas about Jesus are still floating around in our contemporary world. Arius has many intellectual descendants.

New Age devotees honor Jesus as a mystical sage who once traveled to the Far East to learn Hindu teachings. Muslims honor Jesus as just one prophet in a long line of prophets culminating in Mohammed, the true and final prophet of Allah. Meanwhile, as we have seen, the Jesus Seminar claims that Jesus is no more than a long-dead teacher. Not surprisingly the Jesus Seminar does not regard the creeds very highly. It goes so far as to say that the real Jesus is *smothered* by documents like the Apostles' and Nicene creeds.

In our look at the Apostles' Creed we noted that it ought to be said slowly, honoring the years of careful, prayerful thought that went into it, and recognizing the powerfully rich theology that lies behind its various articles. That is also true of the Nicene Creed. Confessing that Jesus is "of the same essence as the Father" should cause a catch in our breath and a quickening of our pulse. It should do so in anyone who honors and worships Jesus as the true and eternal Son of God, who finds salvation through his life and work, and who truly expects this same risen Jesus to return on clouds of glory to bring us to our eternal home. For tucked into that article is either the rarest of theological gems or the most hideous of historical deceptions.

Being an orthodox believer means embracing that first possibility. It also means that we confess such a belief with awe and maybe a bit of holy trembling, two commodities that are increasingly rare in our modern world. At the same time it seems that a true and right biblical understanding of Jesus is also becoming rare. Perhaps there is a connection between the two.

The gospel writer John tells how patiently Jesus leads his disciples to a full understanding of who he really is. A lot has to happen before Thomas finally "gets it":

[27]Then [Jesus] said to Thomas, "Put your finger here; see my hands. Reach out your hand and put it into my side. Stop doubting and believe."

[28]Thomas said to him, "My Lord and my God!" (John 20:27-28).

Some die-hard modern-day Arians insist that Thomas was not making a confession about Jesus' divinity here at all. They take him to be so astonished at seeing Jesus in the flesh that he is swearing. But if that's the case, Jesus' response makes no sense at all:

[29]Then Jesus told him, "Because you have seen me, you have believed; blessed are those who have not seen and yet have believed" (John 20:29).

NOTABLE LINES

As with the Apostles' Creed, the scope of this brief study does not allow us to dissect each segment of the Nicene Creed. But we can hit a few highlights. We have already lingered over the section that establishes the divine and eternal identity of Jesus, the Christ. Following this section comes the lengthiest part of the creed, which deals with the life and ministry of Jesus. In this section the Nicene Creed closely resembles its cousin, the Apostles' Creed. It includes yet another reference to Pontius Pilate.

One line that ought to be properly puzzling to the careful reader and reciter of the Nicene Creed is this: "And we believe in the Holy Spirit, the Lord . . ." Why is the Holy Spirit called "Lord" if we confess at the heart of our faith that "*Jesus* is Lord"? Does this mean that Jesus and the Spirit are essentially the same person? And if so, does this make God a holy bi-unity instead of a trinity? This insertion seems rather odd and confusing. It's difficult to know precisely what lies behind it.

Although the Nicene Creed does not come with footnoted Bible passages, there is at least one New Testament passage that also seems to identify the Holy Spirit as Lord. In 2 Corinthians 3:17 Paul writes, "Now the Lord is the Spirit, and where the Spirit of the Lord is, there is freedom." As far as we can tell, Paul does not intend to deny that *Jesus* is Lord, nor does he mean that Jesus and the Spirit are the *same person*. That would deny the distinction of persons within God that is key to the orthodox teaching on the Trinity. Rather, Paul only intends to affirm that the Holy Spirit is our living connection to our Lord. Jesus is now on the throne of heaven. Since Pentecost the Holy Spirit has taken up residence in our hearts. So the Spirit is the live wire who conducts the power of our living Lord Jesus into the circuitry of our hearts. During these latter times when we are on earth and Jesus is in heaven, the Spirit is the Lord for us by connecting us to Christ. So when the Nicene Creed calls the Holy Spirit "the Lord," it likely means that the Spirit brings our Lord to us in a living, dynamic way.

Different religious traditions have very different views of who Jesus is. Islam teaches that Jesus was a messenger from Allah. However, it considers the confession that Jesus is the Son of God, who shares in the divine nature, to be a mistaken, later addition to the Christian faith. In this context it's also interesting to search out the views of Judaism, liberalism, Mormonism and the Jehovah's Witnesses. All present very different pictures from that confessed in the Nicene Creed.

SENT BY THE FATHER AND THE SON

Following closely on this line is the article that says that the Holy Spirit "proceeds from the Father and the Son." Those last words, "and the Son," form only a single word in Latin (*filioque*). It's striking that they have been a major point of controversy in history. Believers in Western Europe became convinced that the Bible teaches that both the Father and the Son send forth the Spirit to do various tasks. Believers in the Eastern part of the church detested that notion, believing that only the Father sends forth the Spirit. They considered the words "and the Son" just plain wrong.

We may admit that this is a technical point that in no way threatens the fully divine personhood of the Holy Spirit, regardless of which approach we favor. In spite of that, the controversy over this one word pulled apart the worldwide church. In A.D. 1054, the Eastern (Orthodox) half of the church split off from the Western (Catholic) half in a rift, which persists to this day. That a schism could occur over such a small point involving a single Latin word is an unhappy legacy. It's a poignantly sad example of the often fractured history of the church of Christ.

On the other hand, this split also points to an era when people still weighed the power of words, recognizing that they do make a difference. In a visual age, when our ability to appreciate words seems to be atrophying like an unused muscle, we should emulate the nobler aspects of the former era. Each time we recite the Nicene Creed, we should weigh, enunciate, and think carefully about the words we speak. Those words make all the difference in the world—for time and eternity.

About the Holy Spirit, Gregory of Nazianzus (A.D. 329-389) confessed this:

[The Spirit] always existed, and exists, and always will exist, who neither had a beginning, nor will have an end . . .

ever being partaken, but not partaking;

perfecting, not being perfected;

sanctifying, not being sanctified;

deifying, not being deified . . .

Life and Lifegiver;

Light and Lightgiver;

absolute Good, and Spring of Goodness . . .

by Whom the Father is known and the Son is glorified . . .

—*Orations*, XLI.9

R E F L E C T I O N S

▶ *Points to Ponder*

[The Jesus Seminar scholars'] procedures are so influenced by these biases that the Seminar's conclusions of necessity echo their presuppositions.

A good thing resulting from this debate is that people are forced to ponder afresh what Christians have always known to be the key issue: the true origin and identity of Jesus.

Christians past and present have no business worshiping Jesus if he is not "God from God, Light from Light, true God from true God." If Jesus is just another creature like angels, humans, or hummingbirds, then Christians have reason to doubt whether he was actually strong enough to take on sin and the devil—to pull off the cosmic feat of achieving our salvation.

So the Spirit is the live wire who conducts the power of our living Lord Jesus into the circuitry of our hearts.

We should weigh, enunciate, and think carefully about the words we speak each time we recite the Nicene Creed. Those words make all the difference in the world—for time and eternity.

▶ Implications and Applications

1. What are the deepest, most basic assumptions you have that determine the way you see the world?

2. What difference does it make in your life if Jesus is really God or not?

3. Which passages of Scripture indicate clearly that Jesus is God?

4. Compare the differences between the Nicene and the Apostles' creeds. What accounts for these differences?

5. How should we respond to people today who do not believe that Jesus is God?

ATHANASIAN CREED

*Whoever desires to be saved should above all
hold to the catholic faith.
Anyone who does not keep it whole and unbroken
will doubtless perish eternally.*

Now this is the catholic faith:

> *That we worship one God in trinity
> and the trinity in unity,
> neither blending their persons
> nor dividing their essence.*
>> *For the person of the Father is a distinct person,
>> the person of the Son is another,
>> and that of the Holy Spirit still another.
>> But the divinity of the Father, Son, and Holy Spirit is one,
>> their glory equal, their majesty coeternal.*

> *What quality the Father has, the Son has, and the Holy
> Spirit has.
> The Father is uncreated,
> the Son is uncreated,
> the Holy Spirit is uncreated.*

> *The Father is immeasurable,
> the Son is immeasurable,
> the Holy Spirit is immeasurable.*

> *The Father is eternal,
> the Son is eternal,
> the Holy Spirit is eternal.*

>> *And yet there are not three eternal beings;
>> there is but one eternal being.
>> So too there are not three uncreated or
>> immeasurable beings;
>> there is but one uncreated and immeasurable being.*

Similarly, the Father is almighty,
the Son is almighty,
the Holy Spirit is almighty.
   Yet there are not three almighty beings;
   there is but one almighty being.

Thus the Father is God,
the Son is God,
the Holy Spirit is God.
   Yet there are not three gods;
   there is but one God.

Thus the Father is Lord,
the Son is Lord,
the Holy Spirit is Lord.
   Yet there are not three lords;
   there is but one Lord.

Just as Christian truth compels us
to confess each person individually
as both God and Lord,
so catholic religion forbids us
to say that there are three gods or lords.

The Father was neither made nor created nor begotten
   from anyone.
The Son was neither made nor created;
he was begotten from the Father alone.
The Holy Spirit was neither made nor created nor begotten;
he proceeds from the Father and the Son.

Accordingly there is one Father, not three fathers;
there is one Son, not three sons;
there is one Holy Spirit, not three holy spirits.

Nothing in this trinity is before or after,
nothing is greater or smaller;
in their entirety the three persons
are coeternal and coequal with each other.

So in everything, as was said earlier,
we must worship their trinity in their unity
and their unity in their trinity.

Anyone then who desires to be saved
should think thus about the trinity.

But it is necessary for eternal salvation
that one also believe in the incarnation
of our Lord Jesus Christ faithfully.

Now this is the true faith:

That we believe and confess
that our Lord Jesus Christ, God's Son,
is both God and human, equally.

He is God from the essence of the Father,
begotten before time;
and he is human from the essence of his mother,
born in time;
completely God, completely human,
with a rational soul and human flesh;
equal to the Father as regards divinity,
less than the Father as regards humanity.

Although he is God and human,
yet Christ is not two, but one.
He is one, however,
not by his divinity being turned into flesh,
but by God's taking humanity to himself.

He is one,
certainly not by the blending of his essence,
but by the unity of his person.
For just as one human is both rational soul and flesh,
so too the one Christ is both God and human.

He suffered for our salvation;
he descended to hell;
he arose from the dead;
he ascended to heaven;
he is seated at the Father's right hand;

from there he will come to judge the living and the dead.
At his coming all people will arise bodily
and give an accounting of their own deeds.
Those who have done good will enter eternal life,
and those who have done evil will enter eternal fire.

This is the catholic faith:
one cannot be saved without believing it firmly and faithfully.

THE
ATHANASIAN CREED
The Creed to End All Creeds?

I

t's not difficult to see why we seldom use the Athanasian Creed in public worship. A stately reading of the Apostles' Creed takes about forty-five seconds. A proper reading of the Nicene Creed lasts about a minute. But even a moderately paced recital of the Athanasian Creed requires at least five minutes!

It's not just sheer length that prevents us from slotting this third ecumenical creed into our liturgies. It's mainly the creed's content and wording that makes us shy away. Not only is the Athanasian Creed far and away the longest of our creeds, it's also the most theologically precise and scholastically elaborate. When we first read it we may find it tedious. As we examine it more closely its wordiness may even irritate us!

What's the background and purpose of this wordy creed? We know little about it. No one knows who composed it. It certainly was *not* the theologian for whom it is named:

Athanasius. This fact has prompted the old barb that the Athanasian Creed is neither by Athanasius nor is it a creed.

As bishop of Alexandria from A.D. 328 to 373, Athanasius was a staunch foe of Arius and other heretics whose teachings on the Trinity and the nature of Christ deviated from biblical orthodoxy. So the content of this creed would certainly have met with Athanasius's approval. But it is now widely believed that this creed was not written until close to two hundred years after the bishop's death.

IF THIS IS BRIEF AND MEMORABLE . . .

In spite of this, and in spite of its dissimilarity to the other two creeds we've considered, this document is creedal in every significant sense. Its purpose—believe it or not—is to summarize the teachings of Scripture in a brief and memorable form. The creed's two topics are the doctrines of the Trinity and of the incarnation, of Jesus' coming in the flesh.

Anyone who has ever visited a theological library knows that shelf after shelf is crammed with thick, fusty, intimidating volumes on these two complex subjects. That someone in the early years of the sixth century was able to condense all of that vital complexity into a creed of a scant forty-four verses is an amazing theological achievement. Some scholars believe that the intended audience for this creed was the clergy. It would serve them as a kind of theological primer, educating them in these two vital, dicey areas of the faith. Seminarians memorized such a statement as part of their theological education. Later on, as ministers, they recalled it to insure that their sermons measured up to the standards of orthodoxy. As a concise summary of the doctrines of the Trinity and the incarnation, the Athanasian Creed helped many a pastor in the ancient world. Today it endures as what someone once called "one of the most splendid legacies of the patristic age."

THE ATHANASIAN CREED TODAY

If you are not a professional theologian or pastor, and if crawling around in dusty nooks of academia is not your idea of a good time, of what use is the Athanasian Creed to you?

Like the other two creeds, the Athanasian Creed can remind you of what sound Christian teaching looks like. It can help you spy out unsound counterfeits you may run across on today's information superhighway.

We may be a bit put off by the creed's opening and closing lines, which promise sure damnation to anyone who doesn't understand and keep the truths it expounds. However, it really *does* nail down the basics of Christian orthodoxy. In our age too many people dispense with *orthodoxy* (right teaching) in favor of *orthopathy* (right emotions). They substitute emotional gush-fests and spine-tingling liturgical experiences for biblical thought and articulation. In that climate an occasional swift kick to the brain like the one this creed provides may lend some needed counterbalance.

For this reason we'll consider both topics that the creed treats at length. We'll see how even a moderately thoughtful study can clear up some still-popular but wide-of-the-mark conceptions we may have about the Trinity and Jesus' incarnation.

THE TRINITY

Sadly, the clearest and most readily understandable analogies we think up to explain the Trinity are often incorrect. When they ask mom or dad what the Trinity is like, many children get this answer: "Well, Billy, picture the Trinity as being like the President of the United States. Mr. Clinton is the husband of Mrs. Clinton, the father of Chelsea, and the President all at the same time. Husband, father, president—three in one."

This is a clear analogy. On the surface it seems to capture well the dynamic of threeness existing in oneness. It even seems to satisfy the article from the Athanasian Creed which insists, "we worship one God in trinity and the trinity in unity." So this analogy will make us picture God as having three different roles to fulfill, three different hats to wear. One moment God is the Father, providentially superintending the growth of coral reefs and sending rain onto a farmer's wheat fields. Then he turns around and he's the Son, redemptively being born of the virgin Mary or telling a parable on a sunny slope in Galilee. Then he shucks that role to be the Holy Spirit, buzzing around

The Athanasian Creed was probably written in the fifth century. By that time the trinitarian disputes had moved from focusing upon who Jesus is to the question of who the Holy Spirit is. Of course, such disputes are rarely that tidy. Often the debates about the person of the Holy Spirit revisited the earlier arguments about the nature of Christ. Those arguments went hand in hand. Because of this the Athanasian Creed uses much of the same language to describe the Son and the Spirit. That may seem repetitious to us, but it was crucial for a solid understanding of who God is. The understanding of the Trinity described in the Athanasian Creed finally won the day—and the next fifteen hundred years of Christian theology as well. It required more than a little help from the civil authorities. The Roman emperors had to intervene directly to put to rest the widespread civil turmoil these disputes kept provoking.

giving out spiritual gifts, cultivating the fruit of the Spirit in people's hearts, and winging a million prayers heavenward. If all of that seems like a lot to juggle, not to worry: he *is*, after all, Almighty God.

The Athanasian Creed makes clear that the problem with our president analogy is that it is heretical. It teaches Modalism, a false doctrine that washes out the claim that in God we have three distinct and real persons. In the analogy, God, like President Clinton, becomes just one person who fulfills three different roles or modes. But as the Athanasian Creed asserts, orthodox Christianity has ruled out of bounds "the blending [of] their persons . . . the person of the Father is a distinct person, the person of the Son is another, and that of the Holy Spirit still another."

Modalist views were widespread and resoundingly rejected by the creeds. One form of modalism was called *patripassionism.* This belief held that since Father, Son, and Spirit are only different *modes* by which the one God is made known to us, it was as much the Father who hung on the cross as it was Jesus. This runs counter to the biblical view that clearly differentiates between the Father who *sends* the Son, and Christ, who *is* the Son who dies on the cross according to the Father's will.

DISTINCT PERSONS

Somehow our picture of the Trinity needs to allow for three persons, each of whom is distinct from the other two and each of whom does different things. The creed helps us confess that the Son is begotten, not the Father or the Spirit. We confess that the Spirit proceeds from the Father and the Son, but not that the Father or the Son proceeds from the Spirit. Within the Trinity there is a difference in the interactions of these persons.

There's also a difference in how they share and parcel out their work. For instance, while the Son of God in human form was being nourished in Mary's uterus, the persons of the Father and the Spirit were not—only the second person of the Trinity was. Similarly, while the Holy Spirit is busily gifting believers and cultivating spiritual fruit during this age of the church, the Father and the Son are doing other things. Of course, each of the three persons is always aware of what the other two are doing. They never work at cross purposes. They always work in perfectly loving tandem. So the orthodox doctrine of the Trinity as defined by the Athanasian Creed insists on three distinct persons.

YET ONLY ONE GOD

This raises the next question: how can we believe in three distinct persons within the Trinity without also believing in three separate gods? That would make us guilty of the heresy of tritheism. We have difficulty speaking of three persons because in our experience one person is always a separate entity from other persons. You're a person. I'm a person, and our mutual friend is a person. We're all human beings. But we are three *separate* human beings—three individuals. So we might naturally assume that the three persons in the Trinity are separated out into three different gods. We might conclude that the three persons of the Trinity share "Godness" in the same way three human persons share a common humanity.

To such a conclusion the Athanasian Creed provides a resounding *no!* It goes to great, even tedious lengths to teach us differently. Though we are always talking about three persons, the threeness of God is bound up in a fundamental unity. This unity keeps the three so tightly together that we can speak of only *one* God. To emphasize this reality the creed repeatedly uses balanced lines.

> The Father is uncreated,
> the Son is uncreated,
> the Holy Spirit is uncreated.

> The Father is immeasurable,
> the Son is immeasurable,
> the Holy Spirit is immeasurable.

> The Father is eternal,
> the Son is eternal,
> the Holy Spirit is eternal.

> > And yet there are not three eternal beings;
> > there is but one eternal being.

A LESS IMPERFECT ANALOGY

Critics of trinitarian theology poke fun of it by alleging that Christian theologians just don't know how to count. The theologians keep saying everything three times but it always adds up to one. Yet that seeming paradox lies at the heart of the doctrine of the Trinity. "Thus the Father is God, the Son is God, the Holy Spirit is God. Yet there are not three gods; there is but one God."

Coming up with a good analogy for the orthodox doctrine of the Trinity is much more complex than finding a bad one. The "social analogy" of the Trinity, though still imperfect, may be helpful. It pictures God not as one person doing three tasks but as constituting three members of the same family.

Suppose Mr. and Mrs. Jones have triplets. These three children are clearly distinct individuals. Each of them will one day develop a unique personality and a different pathway in the world. Yet these three remain bound together by a common set of parents and by a central genetic link. They share the same DNA. A fundamental unity binds all three together. Furthermore, we can speak of Joey Jones, Jerry Jones, and Jack Jones. Yet we're not talking about three Jones families but just one.

Of course this is still, necessarily, an imperfect analogy. The mysteries of the Trinity always bring us up short at some point. The features that unite the Jones boys pale in comparison to the awesome, divine bonds of love that unify Father, Son, and Holy Spirit. These are so close that the persons of the Trinity literally think each other's thoughts and cooperate so closely that they can never be separated in any way. They are always and forever loving one another as they together pursue their common goals. Each divine person is the exact match and equal of the other two. Yet each one is forever giving way to and serving the other two. As in a terrific marriage in which husband and wife fall all over each other in their mutual service, so in the community of persons in God there is no end to the love, service, mutuality, and adoration that bind Father, Son, and Holy Spirit into the one and only eternal God of the cosmos.

An often-used analogy for the Trinity is suggested by the term itself. A triangle has three and only three sides. It also makes one and only one triangle. You cannot think of the three without the one or the one without the three.

GOD CAME DOWN

Among the most profound and moving of all biblical truths is that the eternal Son of God becomes human. The God who fills the universe with his glory stoops down to become a small—even microscopic—zygote in a virgin's womb.

The God beyond time and eternity enters our time. The God who knows the glories of heaven and who travels at will over the breadth of the universe comes down to walk footsore and weary on the dusty, manure-encrusted streets of Palestine. The God who nurtures all life himself becomes dependent on the nourishment of Mary's womb. The God who is Life itself comes down to die a hideous death.

A real danger in trying to figure out the mechanics of the incarnation is that our tortured, complex theological arguments begin to eclipse this profound beauty. But pondering the ins and outs of this miracle is definitely worth the effort, because the Bible clearly affirms that our salvation results from God becoming a true human being. Somewhere in the mystery of the incarnation salvation has appeared for us.

Just as with the Trinity, the incarnation requires us to speak of a plurality in the midst of a unity. In this case we speak of two in one: Jesus is truly God and truly human. Yet he is not two persons but only one. Within the person of Jesus of Nazareth there is a perfect divine nature and a truly human nature. The Athanasian Creed asserts that these two natures are united in one person. But they are united in such a way that they do not contaminate or change each other. Nor do they mix together into a third something-or-another.

This means that we should reject the analogy that pictures the incarnation as mixing two ingredients in a blender. In that case we end up with a different concoction than we started with, even though it still contains the original ingredients. For example, to make a sweet-and-sour sauce you take vinegar and sugar and allow each to alter the other. Because of their strong flavor, if you pour only sugar or vinegar onto your food you overwhelm and ruin it. But by blending the two and by allowing each to alter the other, you end up with a pleasant mixture that nicely complements your entree. What you end up with is neither just like sugar nor just like vinegar. It's something new.

LIKE OIL AND WATER

That is *not* the dynamic of the incarnation that the New Testament teaches us. A better analogy would be oil and water

Biblically speaking, the word "mystery" is not something completely hidden from us. We tend to use the word in that way, referring to something that we know nothing about. But in the Bible the word applies to something that is *beyond* our ability to know or understand fully. It suggests a reality that we can always know more and more about without ever knowing it all or exhausting its meaning. The fact that Father, Son, and Spirit are one God is that kind of mystery. It's a reality we know something about because God has revealed something about it in the Bible. But we can't begin to fathom the depths of that reality. It remains an eternal mystery.

contained in a single glass. They don't mix. If you fill a glass with water and oil you don't end up with greasy water or watery oil. You get oil and water, each intact, and each maintaining its distinct properties although they are united in a single glass. In the incarnation Jesus maintained an undiluted divine nature and an undiluted human nature. Though they are in very close proximity to each other, the two natures of Jesus do not change one another. They do not mix together into a third something. Each retains its distinctive properties.

The Athanasian Creed points this out very carefully. As the Son of God, Jesus has a perfectly divine nature from all eternity. Nothing in the New Testament indicates that he ever loses this essential nature. He has always been God, and he always will be. But the Son of God has not always been human. He "picks up" that side of his being at a very definite point in time: when the virgin Mary conceives through the power of the Holy Spirit. From then on the Son of God, now called *Jesus,* is both perfectly divine and absolutely human. Both natures are forever after united in a single person. "Although he is God and human, yet Christ is not two, but one."

The confession that Jesus is at one and the same time truly God and truly human raised the interesting question about Mary. Can she be rightly called *Theotokos,* the "Mother of God"? Another general church council was convened to decide. To say that this was a hot topic at the Council of Ephesus (A.D. 431) is an understatement. Three different groups of people ended up condemning and deposing each other as heretics. Again the emperor had to step in to impose some semblance of order and unity. The compromise statement that resulted follows: "The holy Virgin is *Theotokos*, because God the Word was made flesh and became man, and from her conception united with Himself the temple received from her" (Ayer, *A Source Book for Ancient Church History,* p. 511).

FAITH SEEKING UNDERSTANDING

In this study we have discovered that a thoughtful reciting and study of the ecumenical creeds give us a good grasp of our faith. It also connects us to the communion of the saints down through the ages. Despite its complexity and verbosity, the Athanasian Creed does this very well, as do the other two creeds we have studied. In these creeds we can savor the sweet, biblical, theological fruit of the ages. Nourished by it we may grow, as Paul urges us, into full maturity in Christ, our head. Grappling with these sometimes knotty truths helps us to understand more keenly the simple, glorious truth that makes up the very heart of our Christian faith: "that God was reconciling the world to himself in Christ" (2 Cor. 5:19).

▶ *Points to Ponder*

If you are not a professional theologian or pastor, and if crawling around in dusty nooks of academia is not your idea of a good time, of what use is the Athanasian Creed to you?

In our age too many people dispense with orthodoxy (right teaching) in favor of orthopathy (right emotions). They substitute emotional gush-fests and spine-tingling liturgical experiences for biblical thought and articulation. In that climate an occasional swift kick to the brain like the one this creed provides may lend some needed counterbalance.

As in a terrific marriage in which husband and wife fall all over each other in their mutual service, so in the community of persons in God there is no end to the love, service, mutuality, and adoration that bind Father, Son, and Holy Spirit into the one and only eternal God of the cosmos.

A real danger in trying to figure out the mechanics of the incarnation is that our tortured, complex theological arguments begin to eclipse this profound beauty. But pondering the ins and outs of this miracle is definitely worth the effort.

Grappling with these sometimes knotty truths helps us to understand more keenly the simple, glorious truth which makes up the very heart of our Christian faith: "that God was reconciling the world to himself in Christ" (2 Cor. 5:19).

▶ Implications and Applications

1. Why is the Athanasian Creed so lengthy, complex, and picky?

2. What analogy helps you best picture the Trinity? Where does your analogy break down?

3. Did the Son of God exist before he was conceived and born? As the risen Lord seated in heaven at the Father's right hand, is he still a human being?

4. Which of Hoezee's comparisons best describe the way the two natures of Christ are joined in his person: the blender analogy or the oil-and-water analogy?

5. The Athanasian Creed states pointedly: "Whoever desires to be saved should above all hold to the catholic faith. Anyone who does not keep it whole and unbroken will doubtless perish eternally." Do you agree with that? To what extent, if any, can we deviate from the wording of the creeds? From their teachings?